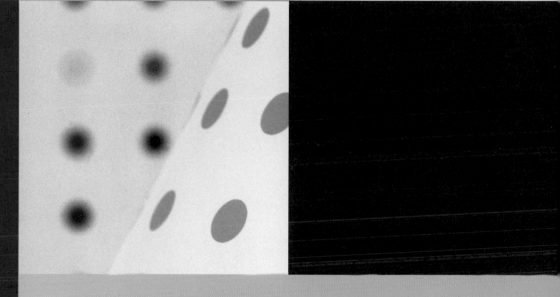

decorating
makeovers

decorating
makeovers

More than **130** easy projects for
furniture, floors and walls,
lighting, and accessories

PETRA BOASE

MORROW

Text copyright © 1999 Petra Boase
Design and special photography copyright
© 1999 Carlton Books Limited

Published by William Morrow & Co., Inc.,
1350 Avenue of the Americas
New York, N.Y. 10019

Library of Congress Cataloging-in-Publication Data
Boase, Petra.
Decorating makeovers: more than 130 easy projects for furniture,
floors and walls, lighting and accessories / by Petra Boase.
p.   cm.
ISBN 0-688-17235-0
1. Handicraft. 2. House furnishings. 3. Interior decoration.
I. Title.
TT 157.B6617 1999   99-42885
745.5–dc21   CIP

Printed and bound in Dubai

First Edition

1 2 3 4 5 6 7 8 9

www.williammorrow.com

contents

introduction

For as long as I can remember I have been obsessed with changing and customizing objects and surroundings. As a child, I painted my bedroom door on a regular basis and revamped any bits of furniture I could lay my hands on. This passion was fueled by witnessing the hard work and vision my parents, a photographer and stylist, applied in transforming the half-dilapidated wreck in the country where we lived into an inventive, cheerful home.

Although I have transformed some extraordinary objects over the years — a defunct computer become a light fixture springs to mind — whatever the project, I always get enormous satisfaction from working toward the end result. It is this pleasure that inspired me to write **Decorating Makeovers**. The projects and styling ideas in this book are for every corner of the home — and they are simple, practical, and fun. From jam jars to old furniture, upholstered chair seats to freshly painted walls, these projects are designed for everyone to tackle — the only qualifications you need are enthusiasm and imagination.

top ten tips

1 Visit yard sales and thrift shops for interesting bargains.

2 Wear a mask and goggles when cutting and sanding wood.

3 Go to ethnic clothing stores for amazing, reasonably priced fabrics.

4 Recycle.

5 Cover the area in which you are painting with a dropcloth.

6 Buy a small can of paint and paint a small area of the surface you want to paint to make sure you like the color.

7 Wear rubber gloves when dyeing fabric by hand and when using non-water-based paints.

8 If you are working with lots of paintbrushes at the same time, wrap the ones you are not using in plastic bags to prevent the paint from drying.

9 Thoroughly prepare the surface you are renovating – whether furniture, walls, or floors – before you start work on it.

10 When painting indoors, keep the windows and doors open for maximum ventilation and wear a mask if necessary.

recycling

My roommate got me hooked on recycling. One day a new garbage can appeared in the kitchen with "recycling only" emblazoned in red paint on the lid. At first I thought it would take too much time and effort, but before long I was addicted to the simple art of recycling. I was amazed at how much waste we crammed into the can every week and also what fabulous things could be done with some of the more sturdy

getting started

containers we'd discarded. The same principle applies if you are clearing out old bits of junk and furniture. Think twice before you consign them to the garbage dump, as they, too, can be rejuvenated and transformed into up-to-date objects – so save your money and be creative.

do-it-yourself

Do-it-yourself is the latest craze. Never before have people had such enthusiasm for working on their own projects, and this is reflected by the plethora of television shows, books, and magazines on the subject,

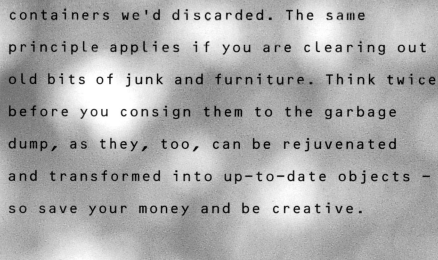

which show aspirational yet achievable
ideas. Whether you are an avid do-it-
yourself fanatic or have never dabbled
before, the following projects will inspire
you to begin transforming every corner of
your home. There is no need to rush out and
buy a long list of tools and materials,
just throw on your overalls and get started.

color

Many people are wary of using color in
their home and do not realize that it can,
if used effectively, create a range of moods
and dramatically alter the atmosphere. If

You'll get the best results
if you take your time, so
don't start a project that
you won't be able to finish;
and above all, have fun.

Take inspiration from these ideas to jump-start your imagination and get your creative juices flowing. Before long you will find yourself pouncing on all sorts of objects and wondering how you can customize them to give them a fresh look and a new lease on life.

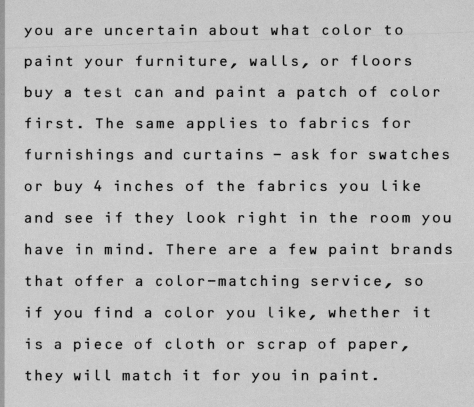

you are uncertain about what color to paint your furniture, walls, or floors buy a test can and paint a patch of color first. The same applies to fabrics for furnishings and curtains - ask for swatches or buy 4 inches of the fabrics you like and see if they look right in the room you have in mind. There are a few paint brands that offer a color-matching service, so if you find a color you like, whether it is a piece of cloth or scrap of paper, they will match it for you in paint.

style

As with fashion, interior design styles and trends can be forever changing - as well as expensive, if you want to keep up with the latest looks. However, if you don't have a big budget there are many ways of creating new looks in your home without going to the extreme of buying new furniture. The answer is simply to alter what you already have with a paintbrush or whatever other tool or material is required. Either copy the following projects directly or adapt them to your own style. There is no right or wrong; all that matters is that you have fun and are happy with the end result.

furniture

Trends in furniture and furnishings are always changing, but there are many **easy** and **creative** ways to give your existing furniture a **new** and exciting **makeover**. You don't need lots of money, tools or a degree in design – you can clean up a tired piece of thrift-shop furniture and give it a new **image** simply with a few coats of paint or a new cover or handles. Rent or buy any tools you need from **specialized** design centers, and if you need to have pieces of wood cut find a lumberyard or hardware store that offers a cutting service. Visit **thrift shops** and flea markets or garage sales, all of which are **great** sources of **interesting** and often **quirky** pieces of furniture that can be **revamped** and made to look as good as new.

kitchen chairs

Old wooden kitchen chairs are relatively inexpensive to buy and can be customized to suit any color scheme. It doesn't matter if you have an eclectic mixture of shapes and designs – in fact, it often adds to the appeal. A quick coat of paint is all you need to unify the set; or you can treat the chairs individually and paint each one a different color or apply a decorative effect like crackle glazing. As with all wooden pieces, before you begin painting, prepare the surface by rubbing down the old paint with sandpaper and then wiping it clean with a damp cloth.

mint & cream crackle

Paint two coats of cream latex paint, letting it dry between coats. When it is dry, paint on the crackle glaze (see page 154). Allow it to dry and then apply a mint top coat. Seal with varnish.

classic cream

Apply two coats of ivory latex paint. When it is dry, apply furniture wax with a soft cloth to seal the top coat. Machine-wash an Irish sweater on a hot cycle to toughen it. Stretch it over the seat and staple-gun it to the underside.

red & distressed

Apply two coats of pink latex paint and, once dry, rub clear furniture wax over it. Paint two coats of red latex paint and let it dry. Lightly rub the paint with fine sandpaper to reveal the base color (see page 154).

glittery blue

Paint the chair with cobalt-blue latex paint. When it is dry, apply three coats of blue glitter paint. Cover the drop-in seat with complementary glitter fabric, securing it to the underside using a staple gun.

black highlights

Apply two coats of pale blue latex paint and let dry. Highlight the design details with a pencil, then follow these guidelines using a fine artist's brush dipped in black latex paint.

For a deep, intense shimmer of color on your chair, make the base coat the same color as the overlay of glitter paint.

tea towel

Simply position a brand-new tea towel on the seat, staple it in place on the underside and cut away any excess fabric. Here, the towel's red stripe has been used as a central feature.

initial

Cut a piece of linen fabric to the required size. Using a fabric marker, draw an initial exactly in the middle, then fill it in by machine- or hand-embroidering in a stitch of your choice. Stretch the fabric over the seat and secure on the underside with staples, tacks or strong tape.

Before cutting your seat cover, make a template by stretching a square of fabric remnant over the seat, allowing enough to turn the edges under the seat. If you are using a fabric that frays, allow a little extra so the raw edges can be hemmed first.

chair seats

Re-covering a drop-in seat is a great way to give a chair a new image. The quickest method for securing your chosen fabric in place on the underside of the seat is with a staple gun, but you can also use upholstery tacks or even very strong adhesive tape. When securing the fabric, work on the straight sides first, leaving the corners to hang. To fit the corners smoothly, cut away any excess bulky fabric and fold the raw edges under, pulling the fabric tight before securing.

mohair

Cut an old mohair sweater to the required size and stretch it over the seat, stapling it in place on the underside. Stick strong adhesive tape over the staples for extra security.

mock-croc

Mock-croc vinyl fabric looks like real crocodile, but is much less expensive and can be wiped clean with a damp cloth. Cut the vinyl to the required size, stretch it over the seat and secure it in place with staples or tacks.

denim

Denim can be bought by the yard and is ideal for creating a casual look. Cut a piece of the fabric to the required size, stretch it over the seat and secure it on the underside with staples, tacks, or strong tape.

shaggy cotton

A new cotton bathmat or towel makes the perfect bathroom chair seat. Cut the fabric to size and secure it in place on the underside of the chair seat with staples, tacks, or strong tape.

canvas & tacks

1 Stretch a piece of artist's canvas across the top of the table and secure it in place on the underside with a staple gun. To get a smooth fit, work on one straight side of the table, then the opposite side and then the ends, leaving the corners hanging free.

2 Cut away any excess canvas at each corner, then fold the raw edges under to get a neat finish, pulling the fabric tight before stapling it in place on the underside of the tabletop.

3 Apply two to three coats of white acrylic gloss paint to the canvas, allowing it to dry between coats.

4 For a final decorative touch, when the paint is dry, hammer small black tacks at regular intervals around the edge of the table.

The table can be wiped clean with a damp cloth, but for more stubborn stains, simply add another coat of white paint.

tabletop treatments

If your tabletop is looking tired and worn, here are a few ideas to rejuvenate it. Not all the projects are heat-resistant, so use place mats to protect the surface when you put hot plates on the table. If you only want a temporary transformation and do not want to alter your existing table permanently, cut a piece of wood, such as MDF board, to the size of the original tabletop and then apply the treatment to the wood. If you are painting straight onto the original tabletop, prepare the surface thoroughly before you start by rubbing it down with sandpaper, wiping it clean and applying a primer. Once the desired effect has been achieved, apply a few coats of hard-wearing clear acrylic varnish and let it dry completely before using the table.

stencilled place settings

1 Apply two to three coats of acrylic gloss paint to the prepared surface, allowing it to dry between coats.

2 Trace your design onto stencil card or acetate and cut it out with a craft knife.

3 Secure the stencil on the table with masking tape or a stencil spray adhesive. Apply enamel paint sparingly through the stencil with a stencil brush. Carefully remove the stencil and repeat, using a different color for each place setting.

4 When the paint is dry, apply a few coats of clear acrylic varnish to the tabletop.

polka dot laminate

1 Make sure the surface of the table is smooth and free from dust. Measure the tabletop and have a laminator cut a piece of decorated laminate to size.

2 Smooth the edges with a plane or sandpaper, then glue the laminate onto the tabletop with a contact adhesive. Weight it down with a few piles of heavy books until the glue is dry.

chess table

1 Prepare and prime the table surface, then apply two coats of white latex paint, letting it dry between coats.

2 When the paint is dry, use a pencil to lightly mark out a border and an eight-by-eight-square chessboard.

3 Use masking tape to mask off alternate squares, making sure the edges are sharp and meet exactly. Paint the squares in two coats of black latex paint, letting it dry between coats.

4 When dry, remove the tape and mask off the border. Paint the border and legs in two coats of turquoise latex paint, letting it dry between coats.

5 When the paint is dry, apply two coats of clear acrylic varnish, allowing it to dry between coats.

1950s-style roses

1 Apply two coats of pale blue latex paint to the prepared surface, allowing it to dry between coats.

2 If you are a confident painter, paint the roses freehand with a fine artist's brush, using blue-green artist's acrylic paint for the stems and leaves and pink for the rosebuds. Alternatively, use a stencil and stencil brush (see page 156).

3 Add small white polka dots in the spaces between the roses.

4 When the paint is dry, seal the tabletop with two coats of clear acrylic varnish, leaving it to dry between coats.

table coverings

These speedy and temporary tabletop transformations are perfect for spicing up any occasion and will definitely keep guests coming back for more. Let your imagination run wild – you can clear it all away at the end of the party. Before you rush out to buy the materials or props for the following projects, look around to see what you already have hidden away in your closets that can be adapted or substituted. You will be amazed at what you find! If the party is not too rowdy and everything is still in one piece, carefully clear away the materials and save them for another event.

spangly sequins

Cover the table with a hemmed length of pink satin and sprinkle on an assortment of colorful sequins. Cover the surface with a piece of transparent PVC so the tabletop can be wiped clean but the sequins stay in place.

red & white

Color-theme your table. Choose a gingham or patterned fabric that color-coordinates with the silverware, dishes, and accessories you are planning to use, and even the food you are going to serve. Drape the hemmed length of fabric over the table.

photo place mats

Enlarge photographs of friends who are coming to your party to 10 × 12 inches and have them laminated at a copy shop. Use the laminated photographs as place mats and wait for your friends' reactions when they sit down at the table.

blackboard place mats

For each mat, cut a piece of $\frac{1}{8}$-inch MDF board to 10 × 12 inches. Sand the edges smooth, then apply two coats of blackboard paint to one side of each mat, allowing it to dry between coats. Place a glass of chalk next to each setting on the table.

Don't throw away your decorated place mats after the party has finished — they can be repainted or simply wiped clean and used another time.

ribbons

This pretty decoration is ideal for an outdoor tea party. Cover the table with pale-colored paper tablecloths and drape long lengths of wide ribbon over the top in a mixture of cotton, satin, organdy, and tulle in lots of different colors. Lay the ribbon at equal intervals across the length of the table first, making sure there is a good variation of color and texture. Then add ribbons across the width of the table to form a grid-like pattern, weaving each one over and under the first row of ribbons. Tie small cookie cutters to the ends of the ribbons to weight down the tablecloth and prevent a sudden gust of wind from blowing it away. The cookie cutters add subtle humor to the overall look, but if you prefer you could try substituting other odds and ends, such as pebbles, shells, beads, or even small wrapped presents.

To re-create this look for an indoor celebration, use a fabric cloth or several layers of sheer fabrics in a kaleidoscope of colors instead of a paper cloth, with the ribbons layered or woven over the top.

chests of drawers

When redecorating pieces of furniture, preparation is the key to achieving a good, professional finish. Although it might seem tedious, spend the time removing old drawer handles and flaking paint, sanding the surfaces smooth and applying wood primer or undercoat. Stand the chest on newspaper or a sheet or dropcloth and don't rush the painting, always leaving it to dry between coats.

silver chest

1 After preparing and priming the surfaces, stand the drawers upright and, working in one direction, paint their fronts with one coat of silver Hammerite paint, which gives a richer finish than flat silver paint. Let it dry for at least 30 minutes but for no longer than 1 hour, then apply a second coat.

2 Paint the top of the chest in the same way, then, when it is dry, turn the chest so you are always working on a horizontal surface. Repeat until the chest is painted.

3 When the paint is dry, attach shiny new metal handles to the drawers.

baby-pink chest

1 After preparing and priming the surfaces, stand the drawers upright and apply two coats of pink acrylic gloss paint to each drawer front, allowing it to dry between coats.

2 Paint one side of the chest in the same way and, when it is dry, turn it and paint another side. Continue doing this until the entire chest is painted.

3 Cut pink vinyl tape measures into 12-inch pieces; you will need two pieces per drawer. Fold each strip in half to make a loop and attach it to the drawer fronts with small nails.

bathroom cabinet

1 Prepare and prime the wood, then apply two coats of white latex paint to the drawer fronts and top of the chest, letting it dry between coats.

2 Paint the remaining sections with two coats of green latex paint. Let it dry between coats as before.

3 To seal the paint, apply two to three coats of clear acrylic varnish, allowing it to dry between coats.

4 When the varnish is dry, attach green resin cross-shaped handles to the drawer fronts. Alternatively, make your own handles from MDF board, paint them green and then screw them on the front of the drawers.

bands of color

1 The color scheme is what makes this design, so take your time selecting complementary colors from paint charts and have them made up in latex paint. Buy a different color for each drawer and the frame of the chest.

2 Prepare and prime the surfaces, then decide on the order of your colors. Apply two coats of paint, using a different color for each drawer front and for the framework, allowing it to dry between coats.

glossy black chest

1 For the handles for each drawer, you will need two strips of scrap leather, $1^{1}/_{4} \times 12$ inches, which can be bought from a tack or shoe repair shop.

2 Mark the positions for two horizontal slots, $1^{1}/_{2}$ inches long, on the front of each drawer and, using a drill and jigsaw, cut them out. Make sure the slots are wide enough to accommodate a double thickness of the leather straps, then sand the edges smooth.

3 Prepare and prime the surfaces, then apply two coats of black acrylic gloss paint, allowing it to dry between coats.

4 When it is dry, cover each drawer front with self-adhesive black, flocked fabric.

5 Cut the slots in the fabric, then fold each leather strap in half, feed it through the slot and tack it securely on the inside.

inside the drawers

Far more attention is always paid to creating the overall look of the exterior of a chest of drawers, with the interior tending to be ignored and quickly filled. However, by being creative and spending some time designing the inside of the drawers, the contents not only look more organized and tidy but the drawers add an attractive finishing touch to a chest when they are open.

striped lining

Measure the interior base and sides of the drawer and cut pieces of wallpaper to fit each section. Use spray adhesive or polyvinyl acetate glue to stick the wallpaper pieces in position.

padded satin drawers

Measure the interior base and sides of the drawer and cut a piece of cardboard to correspond with each measurement. Glue $\frac{1}{4}$-inch- thick wadding to one side of each piece of cardboard and trim it to the edges. Stretch a piece of satin fabric over the wadding side of the cardboard, securing it on the cardboard side with strong adhesive tape. Glue the padded pieces into the drawer.

sock dividers

1 Measure the interior depth and width of the drawer. Cut six strips of polypropylene, making them fractionally narrower than the depth measurement and 25 per cent longer than the width measurement.

2 Mark each strip at 1¹/₂-inch intervals, halfway into the depth. Make a hole at each mark and at each end of the strips with a leather hole punch.

3 Take a pair of the strips and join them together at every other hole with strong metal paper fasteners. Join another pair of strips in the same way. Using the paper fasteners, join the pairs together at the corresponding free holes.

4 Insert drinking glasses into the dividers to check the size of the structure against the drawer width. Make pairs of strips and add them on until you achieve the required size. Remove the glasses, fit the divider into the drawer and insert your socks.

patchwork color boxes

Recycle small metal or cardboard boxes of different sizes by painting them inside and out, using a different color enamel paint for each one. When the paint is dry, arrange the boxes inside the drawer to look like a patchwork of color. Place a different type of item in each box.

After years of never being able to find whatever it was I was looking for in my drawers without making a terrible mess, I decided that the only way to create some order out of the chaos was to group the contents. These sock dividers allow you to easily locate pairs of socks without having to empty the entire drawer, and they can be used to organize other personal items, too. Smaller objects like keys, jewelry or stationery can be stored in a selection of colorful boxes, enabling you instantly to pick them out whenever they are needed.

sailor's knot

This knot was made up at a shop specializing in sailing equipment, but you may like to tie your own if you know how. Use natural rope for an authentic nautical feel, or one or more bright colors for a more funky modern finish. The larger your drawer, the more substantial your knots should be, so use rope with a thick diameter to make a chunky knot. Glue the knot centrally on the front of the drawer with strong contact adhesive.

tassel

Buy a corded tassel from a trimmings vendor. Mark the center point on the drawer front and drill a small hole. Thread the cord through and tie it in a knot on the inside of the drawer, letting the tassel hang down the front.

hole

This hole was cut out with a drill attachment called a hole saw, a circular blade available in different sizes. Mark the center point of the drawer front using a pencil, then align the hole saw with the mark and cut out the hole. Sand the edges smooth before painting the drawer.

stick

Choose a decorative stick or rustic twig for a handle. Cut two pieces of dowel the same diameter as the stick and 1¼ inches long. Mark the position for the two dowel attachments on the drawer front and drill a pilot hole for each one. Drill a hole through the pieces of dowel. Place a screw through each drawer hole and through each dowel. Center the stick between the dowels and continue turning the screw into the stick. Take care not to screw completely through. Once secure, paint the handle.

drawer handles

Jazz up a plain chest of drawers or a
cabinet with inexpensive but original
handles. First remove the drawers from the
chest and take off the existing handles. Fill
in any unwanted holes with wood filler, allow
it to set and then touch up with paint where
necessary. Measure and mark the positioning
of the new handles with a piece of chalk or
pencil before you begin.

jewel handle

Drill two small holes, approximately 5 inches apart,
centrally through the drawer front. Thread the beads onto
a length of fine-gauge sliver-plated wire, leaving enough
wire at both ends to thread through the holes and join
together on the inside of the drawer. When you have
strung sufficient beads, thread the wire through the holes
and pull it tight so the end beads are flush with the front of
the drawer. Twist the ends together tightly, trim the excess
with wire-cutters and secure with strong adhesive tape.

coffee tables

Every living room needs a low table and the following have been designed so that they work as a feature in the space as well as provide a very necessary function.

printer's block

1 Measure the width and length of the printer's block and cut a piece of $1/2$-inch MDF board to the same size for the base of the table.

2 Cut two more pieces of MDF board to make the sides of the table. These should be the same width as the block and the desired height of the table.

3 Holding the wood securely in a vice or C-clamp, drill pilot holes and screw the three pieces of wood together to form the base and sides. Then screw in the printer's block to make the tabletop.

4 Turn the table upside down and screw on four casters, one in each corner of the table base.

5 Paint the table with a coat of wood primer. When it is dry, apply two coats of white acrylic gloss, allowing the paint to dry between coats.

6 Fill the compartments in the printer's block with curios, shells, or any other small decorative items.

7 Have a glazier cut and polish a piece of $1/4$-inch glass to fit on the top of the table.

patchwork origami

1 This MDF board tabletop is covered with squares of origami paper and balanced on two stools of equal height. Decide how many squares of paper you want to use and calculate the dimensions accordingly to work out the size of the finished table.

2 Cut a piece of $1/2$-inch MDF board to this size. Smooth the edges with sandpaper and apply one coat of primer. When it is dry, apply two coats of blue latex paint, allowing the paint to dry completely between coats.

3 Arrange the patterned origami squares to form the design you want, then glue them in place with spray adhesive, making sure the edges butt up to each other.

4 Apply two coats of clear acrylic varnish to seal the paper design, letting it dry between coats. When the varnish is dry, place the tabletop squarely on its base.

When you have glass cut to size for a tabletop, always have the edges polished.

packaging collage

1 Collect and cut up interesting and colorful paper from packaging.

2 Paint the prepared and primed table with two coats of blue acrylic gloss, leaving the paint to dry between coats.

3 Place the pieces of packaging on the tabletop and arrange them until you achieve a design you like. Glue the paper pieces in place using spray adhesive.

4 Have a glazier cut and polish a piece of $1/4$-inch glass to the same dimensions as the table. Place the glass on the tabletop to protect the collage.

floors & walls

As the most basic building blocks of any room, floors and walls provide a **blank canvas** for expressing your style. You can create fresh **new looks** in no time by using temporary styling ideas – simply add an unusual rug to give floors an **instant lift,** and use stylish wall ornaments and crafty hanging methods to give focus to a section of wall. Or, if you feel more ambitious, take **inspiration** from the painting and tile-laying ideas to create a whole new **atmosphere,** even if you only **concentrate** your efforts on a small area in the room. Remember that **colors** will always look different depending on a room's **lighting** and its **contents,** so before you invest in paint, buy a small can and try out patches on site.

wooden floors

Before staining or painting floorboards, remove the existing varnish or paint and sand the wood smooth to ensure a better result. Make sure the room in which you are working is well ventilated, especially if you are using solvent-based paints.

parquet tiles

Wood stain works best on untreated wood, such as these parquet tiles. Use a water-based wood stain in two different shades and alternate squares of color to create a patchwork effect. When the wood stain is dry, finish with two to three coats of clear wooden-floor varnish, leaving it to dry between coats.

silver boards

For a rich metallic look, apply one coat of primer to the prepared floorboards. When it is dry, apply one coat of silver Hammerite paint, making sure all the brushstrokes go in the same direction. Allow the paint to dry for at least 30 minutes but for no longer than 1 hour, then apply a second coat.

Before tackling a new painting technique or other covering for your floor, test the effect on a small area to make sure you will like the finished result.

plaid runner

To cover a small area of flooring, have a carpet supplier cut and finish off a piece of carpet to your specification. Here, a length of plaid carpet has been cut into a narrow strip and finished with a whipped-stitch edging to make a bold runner for a hallway. Other carpet designs, such as animal prints or florals, or materials like natural seagrass, sisal or coir can be used in the same way and look equally good over wood, linoleum, tiles or carpet.

striped floor

These tongue-and-groove wooden boards are untreated, making them excellent for absorbing color. For a striped effect, paint the prepared floorboards with watered-down latex paint in two alternating colors. When the paint is dry, apply two to three coats of clear wooden floor varnish, allowing it to dry between coats. The colorwash gives a similar effect to wood staining, but since it is made from water-based paint the range of colors is wider and the paint can be diluted to a very pale shade or left with a stronger saturation of color. Try using more than two colors to create a cheerful multicolored effect.

To help you paint the stripes evenly, mask them off with low-tack masking tape before you start, using a ruler and a square to ensure straight lines and accurate corners. Apply two coats of alternating colors of floor paint or wood stain, then, when it is dry, protect the paintwork with a few coats of clear varnish. However, if the idea of painting all your wooden floorboards does not appeal to you, try a less time-consuming but equally effective approach. Simply paint a border around the edge of the room.

Because each type of tile is different, ask your supplier for advice on which seals, varnishes, and adhesives to use. Never lay tiles on an uneven surface and always buy a few more tiles than you need in case you damage one or cut it to the wrong size. Sketch out a floor plan to work out the design before you begin, especially if you are laying patterned tiles.

rubber patchwork

Instead of using just one color of rubber tiles to cover a wooden floor, use an assortment. Arrange the tiles in the order you like before fixing them in place, either with a recommended adhesive or by using self-adhesive tiles.

wall treatments

You do not need to redecorate an entire room to change its look and feel. Clever but simple ideas can do wonders for revamping a living space and, best of all, they do not have to cost a lot of money. Paint can be mixed to virtually any color you desire and there are many exciting and unusual textures and finishes available. Not every wall in a room has to be painted to create an impact, either – a color block or decorative effect applied to just one wall or a section of wall is sometimes enough.

modern art

1 Using a ruler and spirit level to ensure perfectly straight lines, lightly pencil a square outline and the positions for the vertical stripes on an area of wall.

2 Mask off the wide stripes with low-tack masking tape. Paint them different colors of low-sheen acrylic paint. You may need several coats.

3 When it is dry, re-mask some areas and paint on stripes of different widths and colors. Start with the palest color, adding richer shades as you re-mask.

When creating
stripes or masking
straight edges
for painting or
tiling, always use
a spirit level to
guide you.

dado stripes

Using a ruler and spirit level, lightly mark a horizontal line on the wall at about hip height. Carefully stick a colored adhesive tape, such as carpet tape, along the line to create the dado. Repeat the process, this time sticking a thinner tape in the same color under the wide stripe.

dot-mania

Brighten up a painted wall with dots. Simply select one or more colors of low-sheen acrylic paint, dab one end of a small foam roller into the paint, then stamp it on the wall. Repeat to cover the wall randomly with dots or organize them into lines or a pattern.

pegboard

This is a colorful way to enhance and organize a bedroom wall or closet. Buy a sheet of pegboard and two wooden battens from a lumberyard or hardware store. Screw or glue the battens to the back of the pegboard, one at the top and one at the bottom, then screw the battens into the wall to hang the board in place. Paint the pegboard with one or two coats of acrylic gloss paint in a bright color. When it is dry, hang fashion accessories from hooks on the board.

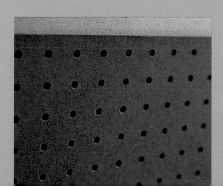

When painting a
section of wall,
mask off the area
for painting with
low-tack masking
tape (available
from art and
crafts supply
stores) to ensure
neat edges.
Protect the floor
by covering it
right up to the
wall with a sheet
or dropcloth.
To avoid paint-
splattered arms
when using a
paint roller,
wear a long-
sleeved shirt.

blackboard

Cover a section of wall with blackboard
paint, either near a phone for writing
down messages or in the kitchen for
making shopping lists, and keep a glass
of chalk nearby. Accurately mask off the
area with low-tack masking tape, using
a spirit level, ruler, and square to make
sure the edges are straight and the
corners are precise. Apply two coats of
blackboard paint, allowing it to dry
between coats.

colored grout

When tiling a wall or floor add color to the tile grout for a sensational effect. Simply choose a color of artist's acrylic paint, squeeze it into the grout sparingly and mix it thoroughly. Keep adding tiny amounts of paint until you achieve the desired depth of color. Remember that the grout will dry lighter than the color of the mixture when it is moist. Once you are satisfied with the shade, use the colored mixture to grout between the tiles, immediately wiping any excess off the surface of the tiles with a damp cloth. Store any unused grout in a sealed plastic container.

When positioning tiles on a wall, mark a straight horizontal and vertical pencil guideline along the bottom and side of the wall, using a spirit level, square, and ruler. Or, temporarily stick wooden battens on the wall in these positions and align the tiles with them.

candy stripes

A spirit level, square and ruler are essential tools for ensuring straight stripes. First, measure and lightly pencil in the stripes on the wall, making a good variation of wide and narrow stripes. Mask off the areas for painting with low-tack masking tape, then paint in the stripes in matte latex paint.

wall hangings

If your collection of prints and paintings is somewhat limited, create your own works of art to adorn your walls and add color. Blank walls can be decorated imaginatively and inexpensively by hanging up painted canvases and frames, arrangements of postcards or photographs, and many other items. Blank canvases can be bought ready-made from art supply stores and are available in a huge range of sizes.

patterned mural

Photocopy a selection of black-and-white geometric patterns to the desired size. Arrange the photocopies to form a design you like, then stick them on the wall with a clear spray adhesive. Carefully align the edges together so they are flush with each other, and make sure the arrangement is straight.

embossed wall

Trace or draw a selection of letters on a piece of $\frac{1}{8}$-inch MDF board. Cut out the letters using a fret saw or power jigsaw, then sand the edges smooth. Apply a coat of primer, then, when it is dry, paint the letters the same color as the wall in matte latex paint, allowing the paint to dry between coats. Glue the letters on the wall with a strong, clear glue, either placing them randomly or spelling them out to make a word. Alternatively, stick them to the wall with strong carpet tape.

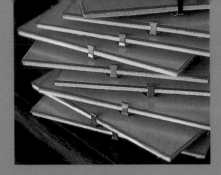

words on a wall

Choose letters in different fonts from a book of graphic typefaces to make up a word, then photocopy the letters individually to the required size. Alternatively, use computer fonts and print them out. Insert each letter into a clip-frame and hang them together on a wall to spell out the word.

If you are obsessed with crosswords and other word puzzles, cover a whole wall with letters in clip-frames hung from picture hooks and move them around to create new words whenever you like.

patchwork felt
memo board

Cut as many squares of $^5/_8$-inch-thick
cork as you need to fill your chosen
area of wall, making sure they are all
the same size. Then, allowing an extra
inch all around, cut the same number
of squares of felt, each one a different
color. Cover each piece of board with a
square of felt, making sure the front is
smooth before stapling or gluing it in
place on the reverse side. Decide
which colors you want next to each
other, then use strong contact adhesive
to glue the squares in position on
the wall, butting the edges of each one
to another.

hanging cards

Tie lengths of string or wire vertically or horizontally against the wall, anchoring them at both ends with screw eyes. Clip a collection of postcards to the string with clothespins or metal clips.

glitzy glitter

Paint two coats of latex paint or artist's acrylic paint in the same color as your glitter on a pre-stretched artist's canvas. When it is dry, liberally cover it with polyvinyl acetate glue and then immediately sprinkle glitter all over the surface. Leave it for a few hours to let the glitter settle and the glue dry, then shake off the excess glitter. Hang the panel on the wall and watch it sparkle. For a patterned creation, paint bold shapes, such as circles or hearts, on the canvas before sprinkling on glitter in the same colors. Allow each color of glitter to settle before sprinkling on another color.

matching frame

Remove the glass from a wooden picture frame, then apply one coat of primer and allow it to dry. Hang the frame in position and lightly pencil in stripes to correspond with those on the wall (see pages 76–77). Take the frame down and paint the stripes using the same color paint as the wall. When it is dry, finish with two coats of clear acrylic varnish. Then, when the varnish is dry, insert a photograph and the glass into the frame and hang it back on the wall.

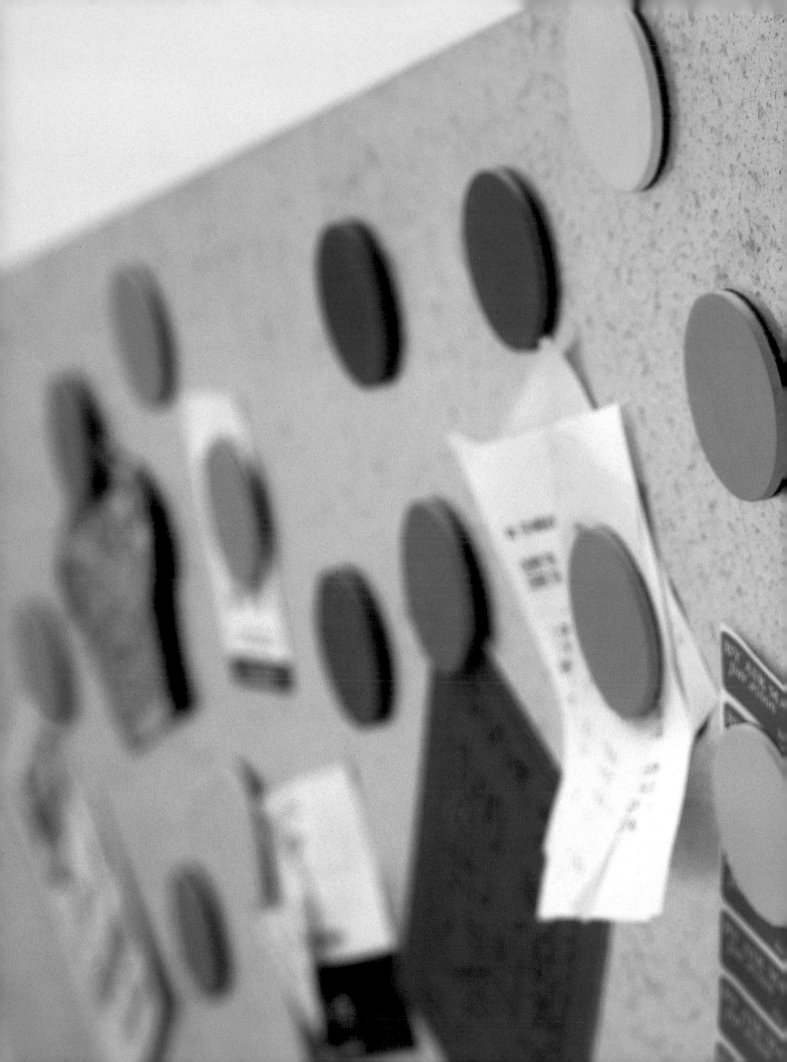

Create your own novelty magnets by buying plain magnets and attaching small objects to them with strong, clear glue. For a fun, lively look, use plastic flowers or farm animals, or for a sophisticated look, glue on small pieces of wood veneer.

magnet board

Using a drill with a metal-cutting bit, drill a hole in each corner of a sheet of galvanized steel. Screw the steel to the wall. Use novelty magnets to attach invitations, receipts, messages and other papers.

cookie cutters

Hang a row of number or letter cookie cutters on the wall by securing them with small nails tapped into the wall. You may want to spell out a name or word. Alternatively, place the cookie cutters on top of a piece of furniture, such as a dresser or armoire.

windows & lights

Light is imperative to how we see colors, forms and textures in an environment. Whether it is natural or artificial, light has a great effect on how we react to a space. Bad lighting can make a room look dull and lifeless, whereas attractive, well thought-out lighting adds warmth, energy and excitement. Candlelight is my favorite; although not hugely practical, candles create the most relaxing atmosphere, both indoors and out. Light diffused through sheer, colorful curtains creates different moods in a room. And when the sun shines through a curtain of sparkling glass beads, the play of light and reflection is sensational.

curtains
& window
treatments

Windows can be made into eye-catching features with a few simple but creative ideas. Spend time looking for interesting fabrics to make into curtains or window dressings. Saris, antique lace, tapestries, embroidered panels, and even 1950s and 1970s retro fabrics can all inspire ideas and give your room an individuality that more conventional fabrics would not. Street markets, ethnic clothing stores and thrift shops are good places to search for unusual and unique material.

When deciding what kind of treatment to give your windows, remember that whatever you choose to do will contribute to the look of your home's exterior.

frosted window

1 Stick self-adhesive number or letter stickers, available from stationery stores, in the desired positions on clean, dry windowpanes.

2 Following the manufacturer's instructions on the spray can, evenly spray window frosting, available at art or craft supply stores, over the entire surface of the windows.

3 Allow the spray to dry, then carefully peel off the stickers.

When choosing the rod or curtain track for your curtains, consider the weight and type of fabric and how it will drape.

striped window

1 Measure the height and width of your windowpane. Then, using a selection of colored sheets of X-film light gel (a transparent plastic, available in self-adhesive sheets), cut out enough strips of various widths to cover the window, leaving small gaps between each stripe.

2 Following the manufacturer's instructions, lightly wipe the window with a damp cloth, then stick the strips of X-film light gel on the glass. As you position the strips, measure carefully to ensure they are straight and parallel.

ribbon curtain

1 Measure the top width of the door frame and cut a length of bamboo pole or wooden dowel to size.

2 Mark the positions at the top of the door frame for two screw hooks to hold the bamboo pole or dowel, then fix the screw hooks in place.

3 Tie colored ribbons, trimmed to the same or different lengths, at regular intervals along the rod. Then hang the rod in place above the door.

4 Tie decorative trinkets, such as keys, cookie cutters or shells, to the ends of the ribbons to weigh them down.

flowery net

1 Cut a piece of pink net to the desired width and length of your curtain.

2 Iron fusible web to the wrong side of colored pieces of fabric, such as satins, cottons and silks. Cut out flower shapes from each piece, either freehand or by tracing around a template first.

3 Working on one flower at a time, remove the backing paper from the web and position the flower right side up on the net. Place a cloth over the shape and iron it to fuse. Do not iron directly on the net, as it will melt. Repeat to cover the net with flowers.

4 Stick a gemstone or sequin to each flower center with strong, clear glue.

5 To make the casing for a curtain wire, cut a length of wide satin ribbon to measure the width of the curtain, plus $^1/_2$ inch. Fold each end under by $^1/_4$ inch and press. Fold the ribbon in half lengthwise, with the wrong sides together, and press.

6 Sandwich the top of the net curtain between the folded ribbon. Pin and stitch along the long edge, through all the layers. Thread curtain wire through the ribbon casing and attach the wire to two screw eyes positioned at either side of the top of the window frame.

Sheer and lightweight fabrics in pretty colors make stylish alternatives to conventional net curtains. They can be casually slung over curtain rods or wire, which makes them easy to switch around or remove for cleaning.

double-color curtain

1 Measure the height and width of the window. Cut two pieces of sheer fabric, such as lightweight cotton or organza, in different colors to size, adding $^3/_4$ inch for the hem allowances on all sides.

2 With right sides facing, stitch the two pieces together along the top edges,

providing a $^3/_4$-inch seam allowance. Press under and machine-hem the six remaining raw edges.

3 Attach a length of curtain wire to the top of the window frame with screw eyes. Hang the fabric over the wire at the join, so each color falls down opposite sides.

feathers

1 Cut a length of sheer fabric, such as organza or lightweight cotton. It should measure the desired length of the curtain plus an allowance for the top casing (see step 3) and a 2-Inch seam allowance for the bottom hem, by the width of the window plus a $^3/_4$-inch hem allowance on each side.

2 Press under and then stitch a $^3/_4$-inch hem on each long side and a 2-inch hem on the bottom.

3 Make a top casing for the curtain rod by pressing under a double hem that is twice as wide as the curtain rod, then stitching along the edge.

4 Hand-sew feathers in the same color as the fabric all over the curtain. Then hang it up by sliding the curtain rod through the casing and securing the rod to curtain brackets.

Curtains made from delicate fabrics or ones decorated with fragile materials like feathers should be dry-cleaned for best results.

tie-dye

1 Tie-dyeing is fun to do and adds color and pattern to any plain, ready-made cotton curtain. Make sure the curtain is clean and pre-shrunk before you start.

2 Pinch about 2 inches or more of fabric and pull it up into a cone shape. Tie an elastic band tightly around the base of the "cone". Repeat this process all over the length of the curtain, adding as many "cones" as you like and spacing them apart evenly in lines or randomly.

3 Using a machine-wash dye, place the dye and recommended amount of salt in the washing machine, according to the manufacturer's instructions.

4 Place the curtain in the washing machine and wash it on the recommended cycle. Re-wash as instructed to remove excess dye.

5 Remove the elastic bands and hang the fabric to dry. When the curtain is dry, iron out the creases and then hang it up on the curtain rod.

glass chandelier curtain

1 Collect an assortment of crystal beads from old chandeliers, which can be found intact or in pieces at antique shops, estate sales, or flea markets.

2 Tie lengths of nylon thread or fine ribbon at regular intervals along a secured curtain rod.

3 Thread the crystal beads onto the nylon or ribbon, making a knot below each bead if necessary to prevent it from slipping. At the end of the strand, tie a secure double knot. Continue adding beads in this way until all the threads are covered.

Try a variation of this novel idea by making a curtain from an assortment of colored wooden beads, following the same method as for the chandelier crystals above.

no-sew curtain

1 Fold a sari or any other hemmed length of pretty, sheer fabric in half lengthwise. Then drape it over the curtain rod so the side nearest you hangs down approximately 10 inches to make a valance.

2 Make sure the valance is straight, then, just below the rod, pinch a section of the fabric, through all four layers, and hold it in place with clothespins or decorative clips. Repeat at regular intervals across the valance to secure the curtain to the rod.

window styling

Windows are the main feature of every room, as they feed light into the space. Protect windowsills from unnecessary clutter and use them to "dress" a room with these simple, clean-looking ideas. If you do not have windowsills, add decoration, such as Christmas tree lights, to the window frame instead.

plants

Plants make lovely, fresh additions to any room – particularly if you do not have a garden – and spiky, sculptural plants lend a particularly contemporary look. Buy as many of the same type of house plant as needed to fill the windowsill. Re-pot the plants into identical terracotta pots and fill the top of each one with gravel or small pebbles.

If the window faces south, avoid creating sill displays that might warp, fade or droop when exposed to strong sunlight. Tropical plants are a good choice in this situation since they thrive in the heat and need minimal watering. To avoid water marks on the sill, place a saucer or small piece of plastic under the plant container.

pebbles

Add a little art to a windowsill by

arranging a collection of pebbles

in a heart, spiral, or any other shape.

christmas tree lights

Christmas tree lights can add style and whimsy even when the holidays are long gone. For an extra twinkle of light all year round, hang the lights around the window frame, securing them in place by hooking the wire over tacks or small nails. For a pretty touch, tie short strips of colored ribbon around the wire between each light.

cress

Apply two coats of enamel paint to the inside of a white plastic seed tray, allowing it to dry between coats. When the paint is dry, line the tray with damp kitchen towels and sprinkle on mustard and cress seeds. Place the tray on the windowsill and watch the cress grow.

Once you have created a display that is simple yet striking, be sure to keep the windowsill as clean as possible. An accumulation of insects and dust will detract from the prettiest of windows.

lampshades

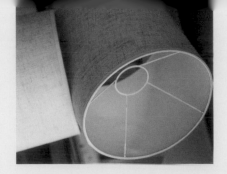

Transform traditional lampshades into something more contemporary and unique with these inspirational ideas. For living rooms and bedrooms, floor and table lamps are preferable to harsh overhead lights, as they add a warm and intimate atmosphere to a room and are more of a visual feature, even when turned off. To reduce the risk of fire, do not leave decorated lampshades on all day or overnight and only use low-wattage light bulbs, 60 watts maximum.

dotty paper shade

1 Using a tape measure and fabric marker, mark the positions for the dots on a plain white lampshade. Add as many dots as you like, but keep them in straight lines and at equal distances apart for a sophisticated look.

2 Stick colored adhesive paper dots, available from stationery stores, in the positions marked.

ribbon slip stitch

1 Using a needle or bodkin, punch holes at regular intervals around the bottom and top edges of a plain lampshade.

2 Thread a needle with a length of satin ribbon, $1/8$ inch wide, and tie a knot at the end.

3 Working from the inside of the shade, thread the ribbon through a hole, pass it over the bottom edge of the shade and back through the adjacent hole. Work your way around the shade, then knot the ribbon ends together. Repeat around the top of the shade.

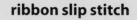

velvet ribbon

1 Using a tape measure and a fabric marker, mark the positions for the six ribbons on a plain lampshade.

2 Measure the shade's circumference at each of these points and cut six lengths of velvet ribbon to size, adding $^3/_4$ inch to each for overlapping the ends.

3 Stick double-sided adhesive tape on the back of each ribbon.

4 To attach each ribbon, remove the backing tape from the adhesive, then stick the ribbon in position around the shade, smoothing it down carefully and making sure it is straight.

felt fringe

1 Cut strips of flame-retardant felt $3^1/_2$ inches wide and the same length as the circumference of the shade plus an extra $^3/_4$ inch for overlapping the ends. Here, 15 strips were required to cover a shade 12 inches high.

2 To create the fringe, cut snips, $2^1/_2$ inches deep, into the strips at regular intervals along the length.

3 Glue one strip of felt around the bottom of the shade, positioning it so that the fringe hangs down below the edge. Glue on the next strip so that its fringe overlaps the top of the first strip. Continue adding strips of felt in this way until the shade is covered.

4 Finish off the top of the shade by gluing on a band of velvet ribbon.

frills of net

1 Cut three strips of net, 8 inches wide and twice the circumference of the bottom of a plain lampshade.

2 Sew a running stitch centrally along the length of one strip. Pull one end of the thread to gather the fabric, adjusting it to fit around the shade. Knot the threads together to secure the gathers. Repeat for the remaining two net strips.

3 Placing your stitches over the running stitch, sew one strip of net to the bottom edge of the shade. Sew on another strip $^1/_2$ inch above the first, then add the final strip to create tiers of netting.

raffia knots

1 With a soft pencil, mark a series of pairs of dots with about $3/8$ inch between them, randomly spacing them over a plain shade.

2 Thread a tapestry needle with a double length of raffia and push it through one dot, leaving about $2 3/8$ inches of raffia, and then back out through the adjacent dot. Tie a double knot on the exterior of the shade and trim the ends. Repeat for each pair of dots.

punched paper

1 Position a heart template on a paper shade and trace around it with a soft pencil. Using a tapestry needle, punch holes along the line to create the shape. Erase any markings.

2 Create another heart outline $1/8$ inch inside the first, using a thinner needle.

mirror sequins

1 With a soft pencil, mark the positions for the Indian-style mirror sequins, spacing them randomly over a plain shade. Stick the mirrors in position with strong, clear glue and allow it to dry.

2 When the glue is dry, stick a short length of embroidered edging around each mirror with strong, clear glue.

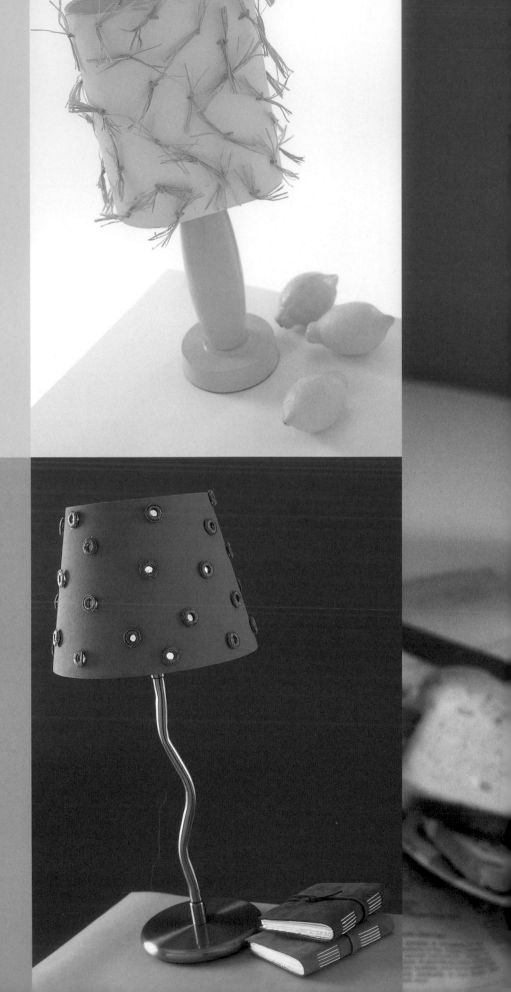

parchment cutouts

1 With a soft pencil and a tape measure, divide a parchment shade into equal-width vertical panels. Trace around a circular template to mark circles in each panel, making sure they are evenly spaced horizontally and vertically.

2 Starting from the center of each circle, cut out each shape along the marked line with very small scissors or a craft knife. Erase any markings.

3 Using a slightly larger template as a guide, cut out circles from an assortment of natural paper. With strong, clear glue, stick a paper circle to the inside of the shade to cover each opening.

If you are decorating your lampshade with materials that are not flame-retardant, apply a flame-retardant spray, available from suppliers of theatrical materials, evenly all over the finished shade.

pink feathers

1 With a soft pencil, mark the position for three equal tiers of wide feather fringe around the circumference of a lampshade. The top tier should be attached flush with the top of the shade and the lowest should allow the feathers to hang down below the rim.

2 Cut wide bands of feather fringe to correspond to the circumference of the shade at each position, allowing an extra ¾ inch for overlapping the ends of each one.

3 Pin the bands of feather fringe to the shade at the corresponding lines to ensure that the shade will be covered as desired. If not, add or subtract a band as needed.

4 Working from the bottom upward, glue the bands of feather fringe in position using strong, clear glue, overlapping the ends where they join.

candles

Whether they are used to decorate a table or simply placed around a room, candles always add a touch of romance and create a sense of occasion. There are so many shapes, sizes and colors available — from tiny tea lights to slender tapers to fat pillar candles — that the decorating possibilities are endless.

bouquet of candles

Fill a glass container or vase with sand and arrange the colored tapers in it, like a bunch of flowers.

twinkly tea lights

Evenly spread strong, clear glue around the metal sides of a tea light container. Hold the tea light by the wick and roll it in colored glitter. Cover a number of tea lights in this way, using several different colors of glitter. Allow the glue to dry completely before lighting the candles.

fruity candles

Choose apples that will sit upright without wobbling, or slice off the base to create a flat surface. Remove the top half of each apple core using an apple corer and insert a candle into each one.

Simple tea lights create a magical effect when they are clustered together in groups on tables, mantelpieces and shelves. Delicate, slender tapers in cheerful colors look prettiest gathered up into bundles in vases, while fat pillar candles are bold enough to stand alone or in pairs and look elegant on a side table. Vegetables and fruit make fun, quirky candle holders for a table display and are sure to be a conversation piece at a dinner party.

concrete block

1 For the mold, cut a base of MDF board to your chosen size. Then cut four walls to surround it, allowing for the thickness of the wood.

2 Screw the walls to the base, butting them together at the corners. Screw the walls to each other where they join to secure the mold firmly.

3 Mix fast-drying concrete, following the manufacturer's instructions, and pour it into the mold. When the concrete is semi-firm, make holes in it that are a little wider than and the same depth as the tea lights. Use a tea light wrapped in foil or a same-sized plastic lid to do this.

4 Allow the cement to dry according to the instructions. Then unscrew the mold and insert tea lights into the holes.

bags of light

Cut two pieces of flame-retardant fabric to 8 × 6 inches. With right sides together, stitch along three sides. Turn it right side out and fold over the top raw edge twice. Repeat for as many bags as desired. Half-fill each bag with sand and rest a candle on the sand.

flower power

Use a tapestry needle to make holes, approximately $3/4$ inch deep, in the side of a pillar candle. Trim the stems of fresh flowers of your choice and insert them into the holes. If you do not want to puncture the candle, cut the stems from the flowers and attach the flower heads to the side of the candle using drops of molten wax.

silver leaf candle

Paint a coat of gilding size on a candle. When the size becomes tacky, wrap a sheet of aluminum leaf around the candle. Smooth it in place with your fingertips, then carefully remove the backing paper.

accessories

From glass jars and bottles to picture frames and mirrors, there are lots of **easy, instant** ways to **decorate** your home. If you are trying to **minimize clutter,** do not panic. The projects are not overstyled or fussy and many are specially **designed** to help you get organized. Anyone who has not yet been converted to **recycling** will see that it is not only practical, but also a lot of fun. With a coat of **paint,** even your empty baked-bean cans can become **stylish** vases, and fruit crates can be transformed into **storage containers.** There are also lots of ways to **revitalize** old mirrors or picture frames and **liven up** three-dimensional box frames.

box frames

Unlike standard picture frames, box frames have depth, enabling you to display three-dimensional objects. They can be hung up or stood on a shelf or table, making them the perfect storage solution for all the small treasures you can never bring yourself to throw away.

silver shoes

Remove the back and glass from a wooden box frame and glue a piece of pale blue felt to the inside of its back. With strong, clear glue, stick miniature silver shoes, available from specialty cake shops, to the felt, arranging them in orderly rows. Paint the frame with primer and then, when it is dry, apply two coats of mint-green enamel paint, allowing it to dry between coats. When the paint is dry, reassemble the frame.

cookie cutters

Remove the back from a wooden box frame. Place the frame face down and arrange small cookie cutters against the glass, then replace the back. The cutters are kept loose so they can be moved around or changed on a whim.

textile art

These handmade felt hearts are chunky, so they work well in box frames. Buy the felt heart pieces or make your own using a felting kit. Remove the back and glass from the frames and apply primer. When it is dry, paint the frames with two coats of a pale-colored enamel paint, allowing it to dry between coats. Cut pieces of neutral-colored cardboard to fit the frames and stick the textile pieces on them using strong, clear glue. Let the glue dry, then reassemble the frames.

silver frame

1 Remove the back and glass from a wooden box frame. Apply primer and let it dry, then paint the frame a pale color using two coats of latex paint, letting it dry between coats.

2 When the paint is dry, apply a coat of gilding size. When it becomes tacky, after about 15 minutes, cover the frame with aluminum leaf, rubbing the sheets on the surface and carefully peeling away the backing paper when it has adhered. Work section by section until the frame is covered (see page 155).

3 Let it settle overnight, then seal it with liquid wax and let it dry.

4 Replace the back with a mirror cut to size and use the front of the frame as a shelf to display objects.

bits and pieces

1 Remove the glass from a wooden box frame and measure the width and height of the inside of the frame and the depth from the back to the groove for the glass.

2 Cut strips of $1/8$-inch model-making wood to make up the equal compartments. The width of the strips should be about $1/8$ inch less than the frame's depth to allow for the glass front. Here, four strips cut to the width

of the inside of the frame and three cut to the height of the frame were needed.

3 With a pencil and ruler, mark where the strips will cross each other, then use a fret saw to cut slots, $1/8$ inch wide, at these positions, cutting halfway into the depth of the strips.

4 Slot the strips together and glue the structure to the back of the frame.

5 Paint each compartment with two coats of different-colored enamel paint, letting it dry between coats. Mark the position of the compartments on the inside edge of the frame and paint it the corresponding colors. Let it dry.

6 Paint the outside of the frame with two coats of white enamel paint. When it is dry, fill the compartments with collectables and reassemble the frame.

mirrors &
picture frames

Old or plain picture frames or mirrors can be simply but effectively transformed to take pride of place in a room. When hanging a picture, have someone hold it in place while you view it from different angles. Careful positioning of a mirror can make a room appear bigger, but make sure you are happy with the reflection it casts. Keep mirrors immaculately clean with window cleaner or by wiping them with scrunched-up newspaper.

candy-foil frame

1 Save the colored foil wrappers from Easter eggs and other candy.

2 Remove the back and glass from a wooden frame. Then apply polyvinyl acetate glue to the frame and cover it with pieces of foil, smoothing them flat.

3 When the glue has dried, apply one coat of polyurethane varnish to protect the surface. Let it dry, then reassemble the frame.

old frames

1 Remove the backs and glass from two old wooden picture frames, then prepare and prime them if necessary.

2 Spray two to three coats of red enamel spray paint over one of the frames, letting it dry between coats. Spray the other frame pink in the same way.

3 For the red frame, have a glazier cut a piece of mirror to the size of the back of the frame and insert it like a photograph.

4 For the pink frame, cut $^{1}/_{8}$-inch MDF board to the size of the back of the frame. Apply two to three coats of blackboard paint, allowing it to dry between coats. When the paint is dry, insert the board and attach it to the back of the frame with small nails.

feather mirror

1 Cut a length of wide feather trim to measure the circumference of a round mirror, plus an extra $^3/_4$ inch.

2 With a fret saw, cut a circle from $^1/_2$-inch MDF board that is $^3/_4$ inch bigger all around than the mirror. Sand the edges smooth, then center a picture hook on the back.

3 Paint the wood with two coats of latex paint, using a color that matches the feather trim and allowing it to dry between coats. When the paint is dry, stick the mirror to the wood with contact adhesive and let it adhere.

4 Stick the feathers to the wood with strong, clear glue, aligning the edge of the trim with the rim of the mirror and joining the ends neatly.

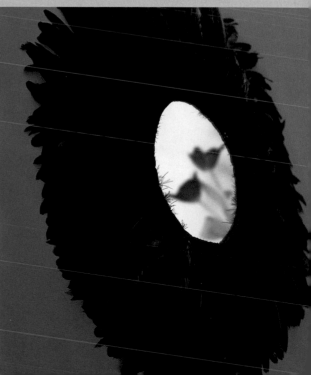

stencilled heart

1 Take a clip frame apart and place the glass, face down, on a newspaper-covered surface.

2 Draw a heart shape on a piece of cardboard, making sure it is the correct size to fit on the glass, leaving a border of about ¾ inch on each side. Cut out the template and position it centrally on the glass with a light spray adhesive.

3 Apply three coats of red enamel spray paint evenly over the glass, allowing it to dry between coats. When the paint is dry, peel off the template and wipe away any residue of glue with a damp cloth.

4 Glue a montage of photographs or pictures on the backing cardboard so they show through the heart. When the glue has dried, reassemble the frame.

i love you

1 Remove the back and glass from a wooden frame. Apply one coat of primer to the frame, then, when it is dry, apply two coats of black glossy enamel paint, allowing it to dry between coats.

2 Cut strong red cardboard to the size of the back of the frame and use double-sided adhesive tape to attach rows of "I love you" tapes. Reassemble the frame.

diamanté frames

1 Remove the backs and glass from two round wooden frames. Apply one coat of primer to each frame, then, when it is dry, apply two coats of white enamel paint, allowing it to dry between coats.

2 When the paint is dry, use strong, clear glue to stick silver diamanté gemstones in tiers around the frames.

plaster mirror

1 Choose a mirror with a wide wooden frame and mask off the edge of the mirror with low-tack masking tape.

2 Mix up the plaster of Paris according to the manufacturer's instructions, then pour it into a rubber ice-cube tray with round or any other shape compartments.

3 When the plaster has set, after 1–2 hours, invert the tray to remove the plaster shapes from the mold and allow them to dry overnight.

4 Glue the shapes to the frame at regular intervals with contact adhesive.

5 When the glue is dry and the plaster shapes are firmly adhered to the frame, paint it with two to three coats of white acrylic gloss, allowing it to dry between coats.

glass containers

Many foods, preserves and beverages come in such interesting glass containers that it seems a shame to discard them as soon as they are emptied. Cleaned up and with the labels removed, they can be given a new lease on life – a row of unusual bottles makes a strong flower display, for instance – while cheap glass vases and bowls can also be customized and styled. For a modern look, paint the containers with enamel or glass paints and embellish them with trimmings. You will be surprised how easy it is to achieve stylish accessories so affordably.

Loosen the labels on empty glass bottles and jam jars by soaking them in warm soapy water; peel off the labels and dry the glass well before decorating. Use glass or enamel paints to apply colored designs with a glossy finish.

wood-effect vases

Measure the height and circumference of a smooth-sided glass vase. Then cut a strip of wood-effect contact paper to size, allowing an extra ³/₄ inch for turning in the top edge. Stick the plastic around the vase, peeling off the backing paper as you go and folding the top edge smoothly over the rim.

WILLEM DE KOONING
Paintings

wrapped bottles

Apply one coat of enamel paint to the top half of a wine bottle and allow it to dry. Wrap the bottle in a piece of linen or any other patterned or plain fabric you like. Holding it in place, tie colored raffia around the bottle to secure it. Repeat for several bottles, using a new color of raffia and tying it in a different way each time. Fill the bottles with water and insert a fresh flower into each one. Group them together or line them up on a shelf.

sequin vases

Apply strong, clear glue to the lower part of a glass bottle, then wrap a length of sequin trim around it, working your way up the bottle and making sure there are no gaps between the horizontal bands of trim. Apply more glue when you need to and, if you like, use different colors of sequin trim to create stripes.

candle-lit jars

Fill an assortment of jam jars three-quarters full with tap water and add a different food coloring to each one. Then place a tea light or floating candle in the water.

polka dot bowls

Stick large white self-adhesive dots, available from stationery stores, to the inside of an ordinary glass mixing bowl, positioning them randomly over the glass and smoothing them in place. Paint the inside of the bowl with two coats of pale pink or blue enamel paint, allowing it to dry between coats. When the paint is dry, apply one coat of enamel varnish over the paint to protect it. Let the varnish dry thoroughly before using the bowl, and do not use it for food products.

colander planter

Line a metal colander with moss and plant an orchid or other house plant in the container. When watering the plant, place the colander on a plate to catch the drips.

metal containers

Before putting empty cans in the garbage or recycling bin, have a look at some of the following ideas. Clean and dry the cans and file down any sharp edges before using them. When reusing metal food containers, make sure the insides are thoroughly dry, otherwise they will rust.

drinks tray

1 Using a bradawl, pierce a pair of holes, 4 inches apart, on one side of a round metal tray and another pair exactly opposite the first. Make sure the holes are big enough for the cord handles (see step 4) and smooth the edges with a metal file.

2 Paint the tray with two coats of enamel paint – purple for the base and turquoise for the sides. Let it dry between coats.

3 When the paint is dry, cut out a flower from a greeting card and stick it in the center of the tray with polyvinyl acetate glue. Apply one coat of enamel varnish.

4 When it is dry, cut two 14-inch lengths of cord. Thread one through the holes on each side to make the handles, tying knots on the ends to secure them.

wheely bin

Turn an old, round, catering-size olive or sardine can into a stylish bin. Clean and dry the can well, then attach four small casters to its base, using a drill with a metal-cutting bit to pierce the holes and securing the casters to the can with nuts and bolts. Alternatively, glue on the casters with strong contact adhesive.

striped vases

Clean and dry several small food cans and smooth any rough edges with a metal file. Then, masking off areas with low-tack masking tape to create stripes of different widths, paint on bands of colors with two coats of enamel paint, letting it dry between coats. Paint the inside of the tin a plain color. If you only have a few colors of paint, mix two or more together to create new shades.

storage containers

Remove the labels from large lidded cans by soaking them in warm, soapy water to loosen them before peeling them off, then clean and dry the cans well. Using a bradawl, pierce a hole in the center of each lid for the knobs, then paint each lid with two coats of a bright-colored enamel paint, allowing it to dry between coats. When the paint is dry, screw on colored plastic knobs.

plastic laces

Using a large-eyed needle or bodkin, thread lengths of colored plastic laces at intervals through a clear shower curtain, tying a knot on both sides of the curtain to secure each lace.

stencilled snowflakes

Add some color and pattern to a plain white shower curtain by stencilling on a design or motif. Lay the shower curtain on a flat work surface. Hold a snowflake stencil card firmly against the curtain and apply pale blue enamel paint with a stencil brush. Carefully remove the stencil and repeat to cover the curtain with snowflakes. Allow the paint to dry before hanging up the curtain.

If you want to make your own shower curtain, choose fabric that is fully waterproof and not too flimsy, otherwise the folds will stick together when the curtain is wet and mold may develop.

shower curtains

Liven up a plain bathroom with a bright and funky shower curtain that will become the main decorative feature of the room. Either customize an existing curtain or start from scratch by making your own. Plastic and other waterproof fabrics can be bought by the yard and shower-curtain rings are available in packs at most large department stores.

hanging essentials

Tie funky plastic bathroom accessories to colored plastic laces, drilling or piercing a small hole if the object does not have a hook. Hang the accessories from the shower-curtain rings.

rosy curtain

Place a plain, colored shower curtain on a flat work surface and glue plastic roses all over it with vinyl adhesive. Use masking tape to hold the flowers in place while the glue dries. Once the flowers are firmly adhered, remove the tape and hang up the curtain.

punched-edge curtain

1 To add a border to an existing shower curtain, cut a strip of PVC the same width as the shower curtain and as deep as you choose. Use pinking shears to cut along the top long edge.

2 Make a cardboard template for the scalloped border by cutting out a shallow semicircle of the desired size. Hold the curve against the bottom long edge of the PVC and draw around it with a ballpoint pen. Repeat to create a series of semicircles along the bottom edge, then cut out the scallops just inside the line. Use a single hole punch to decorate the scalloped edge with a row of holes.

3 Bond the PVC to the curtain with vinyl adhesive and, when it is dry, hang it up.

storage ideas

Tidying up can be tiresome, especially if storage space is limited. But before you rush out and buy snazzy new organizers, here are a few affordable ways to straighten up. Putting old boxes and empty containers to good use, these fun ideas will make your clutter more manageable and brighten up your home at the same time.

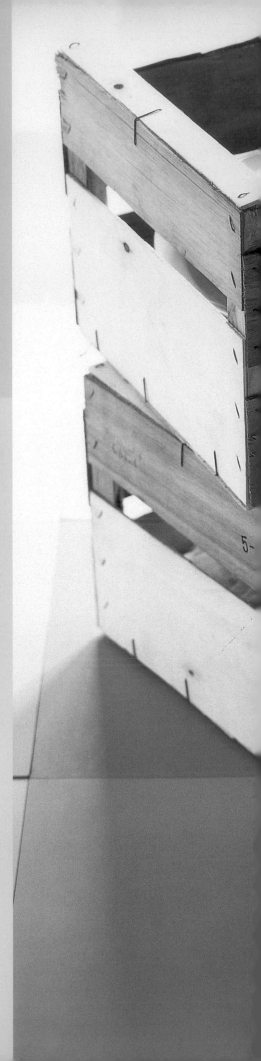

Always measure the items you want to store and the space into which you want the storage units to fit — whether an alcove, under the stairs or a cabinet — before searching for containers of the correct size.

desk tidy

1 Cut a piece of $^3/_4$-inch MDF board, 15 × 7 inches. Sand the edges smooth and screw a caster under each corner.

2 Apply a coat of primer and, when it is dry, paint it with two coats of yellow latex gloss, letting it dry between coats.

3 Remove the labels from four small empty potato chip containers and apply two coats of enamel paint; let it dry between coats.

4 When the paint is dry, glue a ribbon around the top of each container. Then glue them in a straight line to the wood.

fruit crates

Storage does not come much cheaper than this. Collect wooden fruit crates from a greengrocer or supermarket. Clean the crates, repair any loose boards and use them to store everything from cereal bowls to sweaters.

laundry pail

1 Cut out two pieces of spotted red cotton fabric. The length should measure the height of the metal pail you are using, plus an extra 8³/₄ inches. The width should measure half the circumference of the metal pail, plus 8 inches.

2 With right sides facing and making a ³/₄-inch seam allowance, stitch the two pieces of fabric together along both long sides and one short side.

3 Fold over the top raw edge, with wrong sides facing, to create a 4-inch turnover, and press it in place.

4 Make a ³/₄-inch casing for the elastic. Sew a line of running stitch 3¹/₄ inches from the folded edge. Sew another line of running stitch 2¹/₂ inches from the folded edge, leaving a small opening for the elastic.

5 Attach a safety pin to one end of a length of elastic and thread it through the casing. Knot the ends of the elastic together and trim off any excess length.

6 Place the bag in the pail and fold the elastic edge over the top edge of the pail.

camouflage storage boxes

1 Prepare and prime two large wooden boxes. When they are dry, paint each one, inside and out, with two coats of pale blue latex paint, allowing it to dry between coats.

2 When the paint is dry, use a pencil or chalk to draw the outline of camouflage patterns on the outsides of the boxes. Fill in the shapes with two coats of medium blue latex paint, letting it dry between coats.

3 When the paint is dry, outline a few more shapes, overlapping some of the medium blue designs. Fill them in with two coats of dark blue latex paint, letting it dry between coats.

4 When the paint is dry and you are happy with the designs, apply two coats of clear acrylic varnish, allowing it to dry between coats.

filing cabinet

1 If the drawers of the filing cabinet are removable, stand them on newspaper, then clean and dry the drawers and unit.

2 Using a different color for each drawer and the unit, apply two coats of enamel spray paint, allowing it to dry between coats. Work on one side of the unit at a time, turning it over once the paint is dry, so that you always spray the paint on a horizontal surface.

3 When the paint is dry, apply an even coat of spray varnish and allow it to dry completely before replacing the drawers.

Design storage
containers to
suit the decor
of your room,
otherwise it may
look even more
messy and chaotic
than before.

techniques

essential tools

Bradawl A small tool with a sharp point, used to bore holes in wood or through thin metal.

Craft knife

Drill

Fabric marker pen A special pen that marks fabric and then fades, leaving no trace. Tailor's chalk can also be used.

Fret saw An easy-to-use handsaw that is ideal for small do-it-yourself and craft projects.

Hammer

Jigsaw This electric hand-held saw is perfect for the do-it-yourself enthusiast and useful for cutting out shapes from sheets of MDF board and other woods. Care should be taken when working with it, and the wood you are cutting must be secured to a surface with clamps. Always wear a mask and protective glasses and work in a well-ventilated area.

Low-tack masking tape Use it for masking off areas you do not want to paint, and to create sharp, straight stripes.

Paintbrushes Brushes are available in many sizes and with different types of bristles. There are standard decorating brushes, special brushes for decorative effects like dragging or stenciling, and artist's brushes for more detailed work. It is worth investing in good brushes – cheap ones are useless as the bristles fall out. You need a perfectly clean brush for applying varnish, so buy one specifically for this purpose. Always clean brushes immediately after use; do not leave them to become hard. Wash brushes with water after using a water-based product and with turpentine after using an oil-based product.

Paint roller These are available in different widths and textures. Use a small roller for a very smooth finish when painting furniture. Wash rollers thoroughly after use.

Pins and needles As well as for sewing, these are useful for piercing holes in paper and for threading laces and ribbons.

Rubber gloves These must be worn if you are hand-dyeing fabric and when using paint stripper or any solvent-based substances; always wash your hands after wearing them.

Sandpaper Available in fine to coarse grades, sandpaper is essential for smoothing the cut edges of wood and removing old paint and varnish from furniture.

Scissors Invest in a sharp pair of scissors for cutting fabric and another smaller pair for cutting paper.

Screwdriver

Sewing machine

Spirit level Essential for masking off straight lines, hanging pictures or positioning anything that must be straight.

Staple gun A great tool for instant upholstering, such as securing chair-seat covers. As a safety precaution, protective glasses should be worn.

Tape measure

glue

There are many different glues available, but the following are used in these projects. Always read the manufacturer's instructions to check application methods and drying times.

CONTACT ADHESIVE This is applied to both of the surfaces to be joined and left for about 10 minutes to become tacky. Then the materials are stuck together.

HOT GLUE GUN Glue sticks are inserted into the gun and heat up when it is plugged in. The glue is strong, clear, fast drying and ideal for general purposes, especially small projects. You can buy glue sticks specifically for wood and craft use.

POLYVINYL ACETATE (PVA) GLUE This is a clear water-based glue used in many paper and craft projects. When applied, the glue is white in color but it dries clear. Wash brushes in water immediately after use.

SPRAY ADHESIVE This comes in a can and there are different strengths for different uses. Always use spray adhesive in a well-ventilated area.

VINYL ADHESIVE This is used for sticking vinyl to vinyl.

ENAMEL PAINT A fast-drying, non-water-based paint that can be applied to a number of surfaces, including cardboard. It is particularly good for painting metal.

ACRYLIC WOOD STAIN For the best effect, this water-based wood stain should be applied to untreated wood, as it will resist areas where there are any traces of old varnish or wax. Wood stain imparts a rich color, but does not conceal the grain and texture of the wood. Once the surface has dried, seal it with varnish.

paint

There are numerous types of paint on the market. It is your personal choice and the surface on which you are working that will determine the type of paint you should use.

UNDERCOAT/PRIMER All unpainted wood or plaster surfaces need to be painted with an undercoat or primer before applying the top coats of your choice. Once the surface has been prepared for painting (see page 152), an all-purpose undercoat or primer – an oil-based paint with a chalky texture that takes approximately 8 hours to dry – should be applied. Some brands of paint have their own undercoat, so ask your paint supplier.

ACRYLIC GLOSS This is a water-based paint, but it is tougher than latex. It has a sheen, but it dries much faster than oil-based gloss. Use it on walls and furniture. Eggshell paint, an oil-based paint with a slight sheen, is still recommended for interior woodwork.

LATEX This fast-drying, water-based paint can be applied to most surfaces – walls, ceilings and wooden furniture. If applied to furniture, protect the surface with varnish. It can also be used as a base for decorative paint finishes or watered down to make a colorwash.

varnishes and waxes

Varnish is a clear finish that is applied over a surface for protection. There are different types of varnish with different durabilities, and brands may vary in application and result.

POLYURETHANE An oil-based clear varnish, polyurethane has a very slight yellow tinge. It is extremely durable and versatile and can be applied to most surfaces, such as furniture, woodwork, floors and walls. The varnish should be left to dry overnight before applying a second coat. Brushes should be washed with turpentine.

ACRYLIC This is a permanent water-based clear-drying varnish. Buy the one that is specified for your purpose. The varnish has a milky color when it is first applied but dries to a completely clear finish. Brushes can be washed with water.

FURNITURE WAX A traditional solid or liquid beeswax used to polish and protect wooden surfaces. The clear variety can be rubbed over surfaces that have been painted with water-based paint or paint washes to act as a seal, although it is not as durable as varnish. Apply wax with a soft cloth.

preparing surfaces

All surfaces should be clean, dry and sound before decorating, and new plaster or wood must be treated with an appropriate primer. For a wooden surface, remove any peeling paint by chemical stripping or sanding, make sure the surface is smooth, then wipe it clean. For a plaster surface, such as a wall, clean it thoroughly with soap and water, then allow it to dry. Fill any holes or cracks with ready-mixed filler and, when it is dry, rub it smooth with fine-grade sandpaper. If the general surface of the wall is not in good condition, line the walls with contact paper.

sanding

Any rough surface that is to be painted or varnished must first be prepared by sanding. When sanding a wooden surface, always work in the direction of the grain. For most purposes, sanding is done by hand, but an electric sander can be used on large surfaces and a specialty sander for floors can be rented from many hardware stores. Wear a mask and goggles at all times and ensure the area is well ventilated. After sanding, always wipe the surface with a damp cloth and let it dry before painting or varnishing.

tie-dyeing

Tie-dyeing is a method of dyeing fabric to produce patterns. The fabric is tied or knotted in specific ways so that the tied areas do not absorb the dye. It can be done either by hand or in a washing machine, depending on the dye. Always read the instructions before starting. If you are using a washing machine, make sure the fabric is tied tightly to prevent it from coming undone. Once the fabric is dyed and rinsed, remove the ties and hang it up to dry.

sewing

The sewing techniques used in these projects are fairly basic, but here are a few guidelines to help you with hems and seams. A hem is created along a raw edge of fabric by folding under the edge once or twice. The edge is then machine-stitched or slip-stitched by hand. Alternatively, fusible web tape for hemming is available, which needs no sewing – you simply iron it in place. However, I would only recommend using the tape on thick fabrics. Overlocking is a way of finishing off raw edges in seams to prevent them from fraying. On sewing machines, an overlocker sewing foot can be used, or use the zigzag stitch. Alternatively, the raw edges can be trimmed with pinking shears or an anti-fray liquid can be applied.

crackle glaze

1 Choose two different colors of latex paint. Apply two coats of the base color to the prepared surface, allowing it to dry between coats.

2 Paint on a coat of crackle glaze. When it is dry, apply one coat of the second color of paint. The cracks will appear immediately. For a more interesting crackle, vary your brushstrokes as you apply the paint.

3 Seal the effect with an application of clear acrylic varnish or furniture wax.

distressing

1 Choose two different colors of latex paint. Apply two coats of the base color to the prepared surface, allowing it to dry between coats.

2 When it is dry, use a rag to rub a thin coat of furniture wax over the base coat. Allow it to dry.

3 Apply two coats of the second color of paint over the wax, allowing it to dry between coats.

4 When the paint is thoroughly dry, lightly rub fine-grade sandpaper over the areas of the surface that would receive the most wear. The second color of paint will rub away to reveal the base color underneath.

aluminum leaf

1 Aluminum leaf, along with gold and bronze, is available in sheets. Apply two coats of latex paint to the prepared surface, allowing it to dry between coats.

2 Apply acrylic gilding size over the painted surface and leave it for about 15 minutes until it becomes tacky.

3 When it is tacky, position a sheet of aluminum leaf on the surface and smooth it in place with a soft make-up brush, cotton wool or your fingertips. Work on one section at a time until the surface is covered.

4 Either fill in any gaps with more leaf or leave the paint showing through in places. Leave it to settle overnight, then seal it with a liquid wax.

decoupage

1 Apply two coats of latex or enamel paint to the prepared surface, allowing it to dry between coats.

2 Cut out paper shapes and arrange them on the surface to form the desired design.

3 When you are happy with the arrangement, glue the shapes in position with a small amount of polyvinyl acetate glue.

4 When the glue is dry, apply two to three coats of clear acrylic varnish over the entire surface, allowing it to dry between coats.

stenciling

1 Apply two coats of latex paint to the prepared surface, allowing it to dry between coats.

2 Either use a bought stencil or make your own by tracing a design onto stencil card or acetate and cutting out the shape with a craft knife (plastic stencils can be reused if they are washed immediately after use). Spray the reverse side of the stencil with a stencil spray adhesive and position it, or use low-tack masking tape to hold it in place.

3 Using a stencil brush, dab a small amount of a different-colored paint through the stencil.

4 When the paint is dry, remove the stencil and repeat as desired. Seal the finished design with varnish.

plaid

1 Choose three or more colors of latex paint. Apply two coats of the palest color over the prepared surface, allowing it to dry between coats.

2 When it is dry, divide the surface into vertical stripes of equal size using low-tack masking tape. Paint the stripes with two coats of the second color.

3 When the paint is dry, remove the masking tape, then divide the surface into horizontal stripes in the same way, making sure they are the same width as the vertical stripes. Apply two coats of the second color of paint.

4 When it is dry, remove the masking tape and repeat steps 2 and 3, using a different width of stripe and a third color. Repeat until the desired effect is achieved.

gilded dots

1 Apply two coats of pale blue latex paint to the prepared surface, allowing it to dry between coats.

2 Using a circular stencil held in the desired position of the dots, dab gilding size through the stencil. Alternatively, apply the size freehand to create the dots. Leave the size for about 15 minutes, until it is tacky.

3 Cut out pieces of aluminum leaf that are big enough to cover the dots. When the size is tacky, rub the aluminum leaf over the dots, peeling away the backing paper when the leaf has adhered.

4 When all the dots are covered, brush away the excess aluminum leaf with a soft paintbrush.

water-based glaze

1 Apply two coats of latex paint to the prepared surface, allowing it to dry between coats.

2 Pour the transparent water-based glaze into a plastic container, add a little artist's acrylic paint in a color of your choice and mix it together well.

3 Apply one coat of the glaze to the surface, using a dragging brush to create fine lines. The glaze can be manipulated with brushes to create other patterns, such as wood-grain effects, stippling and marbling.

suppliers

3M
Manufacturer of abrasives, tapes,
and adhesives
(800) 364–3577

CHARRETTE/UTRECHT ART SUPPLY
Specialty art and design source
(800) 223–9132
www.utrechtart.com

ECONOMY HANDICRAFTS
Supplier of beads, trimming, sand,
and other crafts materials
(800) 216–1601 or (718) 426–1600,
free catalog

FISKARS SCISSORS
Manufacturer of scissors and paper
crafts supplies
(800) 950–0203, extension 1277

HOME DEPOT
Do-it-yourself home
improvement centers
www.homedepot.com

IKEA
Source for reasonably
priced furnishings,
fabric, and accessories
(800) 434–IKEA, free catalog
www.IKEA.com

JANOVIC PLAZA
Expert provider of paint, fabric,
and other design materials
(800) 772–4381 or (718) 392–3999

MICHAELS
Extensive source of crafts supplies
www.michaels.com

PEARL PAINT
Discount art supplier
(800) 221–6845 or (212) 431–7932

SINGER
Manufacturer of sewing machines
(800) 968–1502

VANGUARD CRAFTS
Provider of beads, ribbons,
woodworking kits,
and other crafts supplies
(800) 662–7238 or (718) 377–5188,
free catalog
www.crafts.baweb.com

acknowledgments

I would like to thank my mum for the use of her house and lovely props,
and Penny Stock for the use of her sunny apartment and its stylish contents.

The following companies were very helpful in lending us props for
the photographic shoot: Graham and Green, 7 Elgin Crescent, London W11 2JA;
Muji, 135 Long Acre, London WC2E 9AD; Paperchase, 213 Tottenham Court Road,
London W1P 9AF; Stirlings, 1018 Harrow Road, London NW10 5NS; and Treasures,
The Old Fire Station, 22 Rous Road, Newmarket, Suffolk, CB8 8DL.

I would also like to thank Sophie Robinson, who has been a huge hands-on support
throughout; Penny Stock for her inspiring art direction; Janine Hosegood for her
delicious photographs; Zia Mattocks for her patient editing; and Venetia Penfold for
listening to my initial idea for the book and for making it happen. Thank you all.

And, finally, very special thanks to Mum, Dad, Marc, and Craig.

index